I0420574

Creative Calm

A Relaxing Color Therapy Book

Volume 1

Coloring is not just for kids. It has been proven to be an excellent way for adults to destress, create mindfulness and slow down from daily life, all while enjoying an activity that you can truly make your own.

There is no right or wrong way to color in the images in this book, and you are free to choose the tools you wish to work with. Markers, paint, colored pencils, pens – the choices are unlimited.

Sit back and unwind and let your stress melt away while you spread color across the page. All pages are single sided to avoid bleed through.

Relax and enjoy book one of this calming series.

Cut out this page and insert behind the page you are currently coloring.

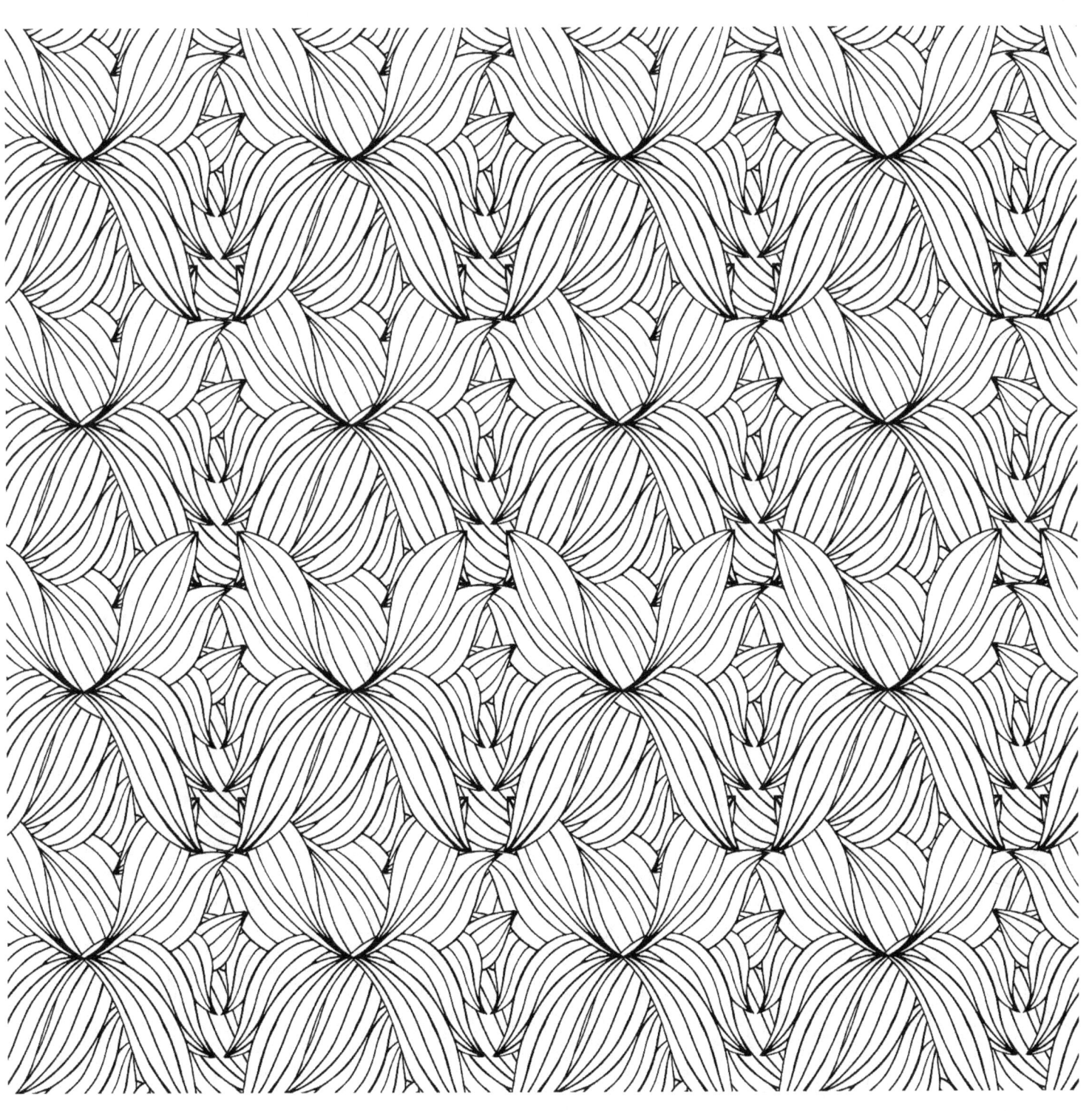

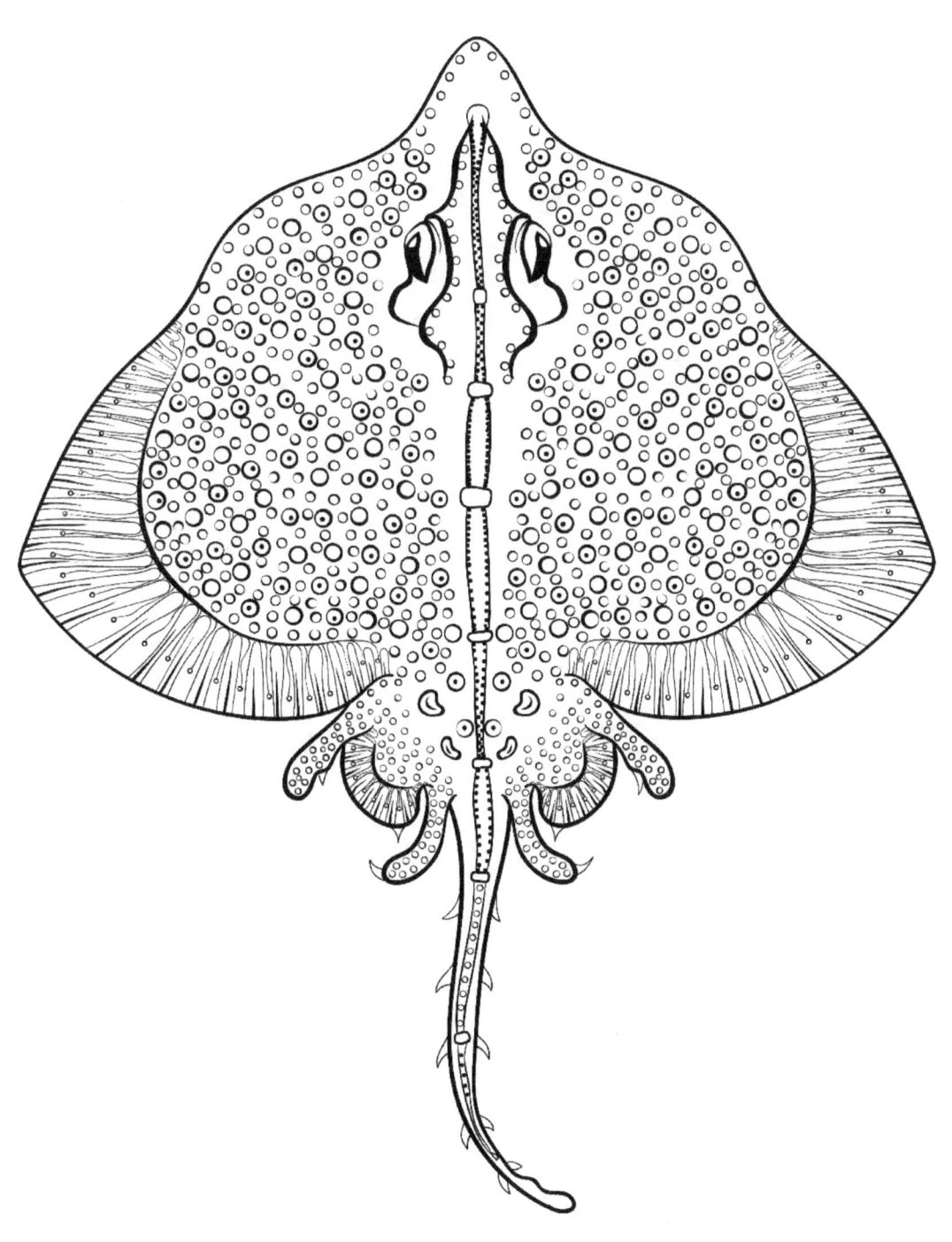

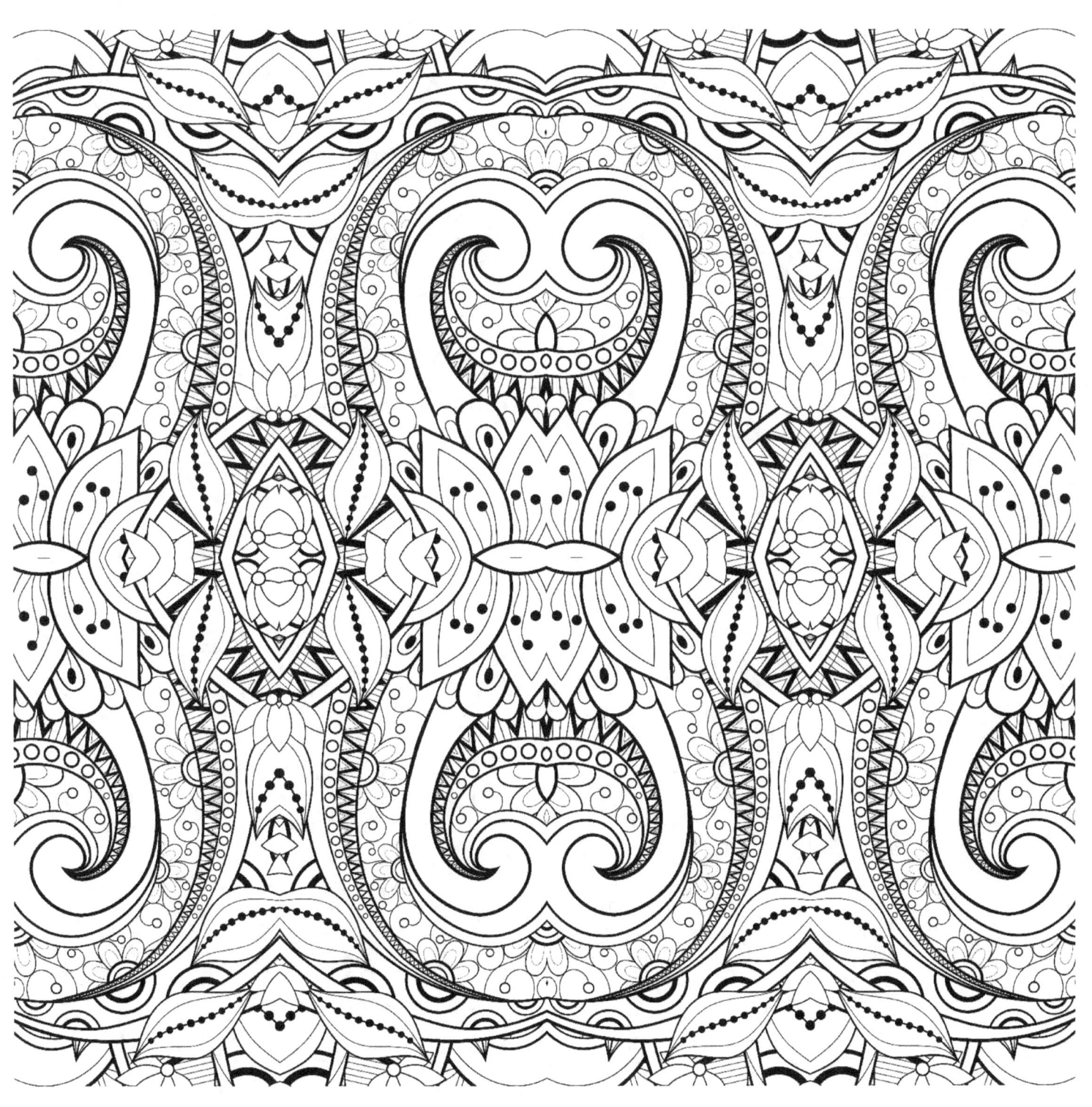